ALTERNATOR BOOKS™

WRITE AND RECORD YOUR OWN SONGS

ANNA LEIGH

Lerner Publications ◆ Minneapolis

Lerner Publications Company
A division of Lerner Publishing Group, Inc.
241 First Avenue North
Minneapolis, MN 55401 USA

For reading levels and more information, look up this title at www.lernerbooks.com.

Library of Congress Cataloging-in-Publication Data

Names: Leigh, Anna.
Title: Write and record your own songs / Anna Leigh.
Description: Minneapolis : Lerner Publications, [2018] | Series: Digital makers | Includes bibliographical references and index.
Identifiers: LCCN 2017006601 (print) | LCCN 2017009247 (ebook) | ISBN 9781512483413 (lb : alk. paper) | ISBN 9781512483468 (eb pdf)
Subjects: LCSH: Composition (Music)—Juvenile literature. | Sound recordings—Production and direction—Juvenile literature.
Classification: LCC MT40 .L35 2018 (print) | LCC MT40 (ebook) | DDC 782.42/13—dc23

LC record available at https://lccn.loc.gov/2017006601

Manufactured in the United States of America
1-43343-33163-6/12/2017

CONTENTS

INTRODUCTION
MAKING MUSIC   4

CHAPTER 1
GETTING STARTED   6

CHAPTER 2
HONING YOUR RECORDING   12

CHAPTER 3
SHARING YOUR MUSIC   16

CHAPTER 4
STAYING SMART   22

MUSIC-MAKING CHECKLIST   28
GLOSSARY   30
FURTHER INFORMATION   31
INDEX   32

MAKING MUSIC

DO YOU LOVE TO SING OR PLAY AN INSTRUMENT? Have you ever listened to a piece of music and thought, *I wish I could make music like that*? You probably can—and it's time to try it!

Beyoncé's polished performances require hard work by whole teams of music pros, but you can make great music even without an entourage!

Sometimes music can sound complicated. There are many different instruments, singers, and even computer-generated sounds. And music does take lots of work to create. Some musicians rely on whole teams of people to perfect their craft. There might be one team writing the song, while another performs it. One team records the music, and still others edit the sound.

Yet the truth is, you don't need huge groups of people or fancy equipment to make music. In fact, anyone can do it. Even the hottest hit songs have only a few basic parts. With just a little creativity and some basic tools, you can write and record your own music— and even share it with the world.

Are you ready to make some music? Great! **LET'S GET STARTED!**

CHAPTER I

GETTING STARTED

WRITING MUSIC MIGHT SEEM SCARY AT FIRST. You may feel as if you don't have any good ideas or feel unsure about how to write a **melody**. But don't worry. With planning, your task will become easier.

Don't be intimidated by a blank page. Just take one step at a time when writing music.

Some songwriters are pros at reading music. Others don't know a bass clef from a treble. Either way, you can be great at writing music!

Every musician writes songs differently. Maybe you want to come up with a tune first. Or you might start with just one line of the **lyrics** in your head. But no matter how you begin, your song will need a topic, or a main idea.

Not sure what to write about? Your song can be about anything! Just look around the room or think about your day, and you'll probably come up with lots of stories and ideas you could write a song about. Write down all of your ideas—they may come in handy later.

Once you have your topic, you'll write lyrics around it. So if your topic is, say, missing a friend who lives far away, write several lines describing how that feels. Put some thought into your lyrics. If you're passionate about your topic and the words you use to describe it, your listeners will care too.

After you have lyrics you're happy with, you'll put the words with music. If you haven't already done so, come up with a melody to go with your lyrics. You can write the melody down using music notes. Or if you don't know how to read or write notes, you can simply sing it into a recording device—with or without the lyrics.

When you have both lyrics and a melody, it's time to figure out something else: How many singers do you want to sing your song? Just one—maybe yourself? Or several—maybe you and some friends who love to sing? And do you want a band to play your song, or would it work better with one instrument, such as a piano? Talk to your friends or your music teacher at school to round up all the musicians and instruments you'll need.

Have some buddies who love to sing? Perfect! You can work together to make music.

SONG STRUCTURE

When you're writing lyrics, it's helpful to know about song structure. Even simple songs usually have two main parts: **verses** and a **chorus**. Verses are groupings of lines that tell your story. For example, in the song mentioned earlier about missing a friend, four lines might describe how much you like the friend. That's one verse. Four more lines might explain that the friend moved away. That's another verse. Finally, four lines could say how happy you'll feel when you see the friend again. That's a third verse.

The chorus is a part of a song that repeats. Sticking with the example of a song about missing a friend, the chorus might be, "And I really miss you, friend. But true friendship never has to end." The chorus usually plays after each of your verses. Keep these parts of a song in mind as you write. Craft verses and a chorus for your song, and you'll be off to a terrific start.

RECORDING EQUIPMENT

NEXT, IT'S TIME TO PLAN YOUR RECORDING. You might be able to record your music with a cell phone. But this recording may not have the sound quality you want. For a more professional sound, find a microphone, headphones, and a computer program. You can buy inexpensive headphones and a microphone. Or maybe your school or a library has equipment you can borrow.

Many music software programs are also available. Find the program that works for you, but ask a parent or guardian before buying, downloading, or using any computer software. Once you have all your equipment ready, test the microphones and software to make sure everything works and you know how to use it. Once you have your lyrics, melody, musicians, instruments, and equipment ready—*whew!*—you're set to record.

CHAPTER 2

HONING YOUR RECORDING

IT'S SIMPLE TO RECORD A SONG. All you have to do is hit the Record button and play the song. But for professional quality, try recording **tracks**, or recording each part separately and editing the parts together later.

First, you'll want to record a scratch track. This means recording as everyone plays through the song together.

When the scratch track is finished, you'll record each part separately—for example, drums, guitar, and then **vocals**. The musicians listen to the scratch track using headphones while recording their own parts. The scratch track helps the musicians play at the right speed and stay on beat.

Timing is everything in music. Make sure all the musicians are sticking to the same beat.

RECORDING

SPACE

Your recording space is important. You need to have enough room for your equipment, but you also want to make sure there isn't much background noise. Find an empty room that doesn't have blowing fans or ticking clocks. Politely ask your family or friends to be quiet while you're recording.

This is a professional recording room, but you don't need a professional space to make a great recording. All you need is peace and quiet. So send your little brother elsewhere!

TIME TO EDIT!

AFTER THE SEPARATE PARTS OF THE SONG ARE RECORDED, USE YOUR COMPUTER PROGRAM TO EDIT THEM TOGETHER. Most programs make it simple to cut and paste the best sections. Then you drag and drop the sections into place until everything sounds right.

Next, make sure there's no extra noise in the recording. Did someone clear her throat? You can cut that out. Finally, you can adjust the sound levels to make sure the piano isn't louder than the vocals or the drums aren't overpowering everyone. Listen to your song again. Does everything sound good? Perfect! It's time to share your work.

Talented songwriters know that listening is key to making quality music.

CHAPTER 3

SHARING YOUR MUSIC

THERE ARE MANY WAYS TO SHARE YOUR MUSIC. But first, decide how public you want your music to be. Maybe you only want to share the recording with your family. If so, you can upload the file onto a social media site, adjusting the privacy settings so only your family can find it.

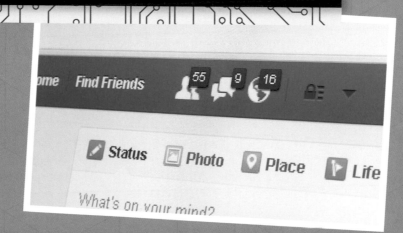

Check with a trusted adult before publicly sharing anything online.

But what if you're ready to share your music with a wider audience? Start by asking a parent or guardian if it's OK. Then you two can work together to find the best place to share your songs.

Sharing your music can gain you lots of fans.

CREATIVE TIP

If you share your video on social media, providing a brief description of it can get more family members and friends to click on it. So much gets shared on social media that it's easy for content to get lost in the shuffle—even if that content is a video of you singing that you know your aunts, uncles, and grandparents would love to see! So be sure to add language explaining that the video shows you and your awesome new band performing a song you wrote yourself.

Your adoring grandparents might find it helpful if you let them know that *you're* the star in that video you're sharing!

ALESSIA CARA

Alessia Cara made her first recording on her mom's cell phone and posted it on Facebook. When she was thirteen, she began sharing **covers** on YouTube. Three years later, the head of a production company saw Cara's videos. Soon she began working with a recording company to write new songs and make an album, which was released in 2015. In 2016 Disney released "How Far I'll Go," recorded by Cara, for the *Moana* soundtrack.

Many websites make it easy to post music files online. One of the most popular of these is YouTube. YouTube is simple to use, and millions of people go there to find new music. Your recording has a great chance of being heard!

BUILD YOUR AUDIENCE

→ **WHEN YOU POST YOUR SONG TO A WEBSITE, THINK ABOUT WAYS TO HELP PEOPLE FIND YOUR MUSIC.** Some sites may have you type in keywords about your music. These terms describe your song. When people search for your keywords, the song you've recorded will come up in their search results.

Violinist Lindsey Stirling has built a huge following on her YouTube channel, which features original music videos, clips of her playing her favorite covers, and more.

Get specific when you choose keywords. The more keywords you use to describe your music, the more likely it is that others will discover that gorgeous guitar song you just wrote!

To come up with keywords, think of the words you'd use to describe your song to a friend. Is your song about a summer beach party? Then *summer*, *beach*, and *party* should be some of your keywords. Does it feature a guitar? Then—you guessed it—use *guitar* as a keyword. Now, whenever people search for your keywords, your song will turn up in the results. The more specific your keywords are, the greater the chances that people will find your song.

CHAPTER 4
STAYING SMART

IT CAN BE EXCITING WHEN PEOPLE START LISTENING TO YOUR MUSIC. It can also be scary. And if you've put your music online, people will be able to write comments about it.

On some sites, you'll have the option to control who is commenting on your music. You may want to turn off comments altogether or allow only your friends to make comments. There's nothing wrong with keeping your music private. What's most important is to do what's comfortable for you.

When it comes to making music, enjoying the process is what it's all about. So share only what you want to share, and remember to have fun.

LISTEN AND RESPOND

→ **AT THE SAME TIME, THERE ARE ALSO BENEFITS TO BEING PART OF A LARGER MUSICAL COMMUNITY.** Being part of a community can help you improve as a musician. Other musicians may write comments on your work that help you make your work even better.

Even pros like Ed Sheeran need to take advice from others to make their music the best it can be.

Discovering amazing music by other artists is part of the fun of online musical communities.

Another benefit to a community is that it can help you discover inspiring work by others. It's fun to see what other talented musicians are up to. And leaving encouraging comments on other musicians' websites can help them to improve as well.

BE SAFE AND HAVE FUN

AS ALWAYS WHEN INTERACTING ONLINE, YOU'LL WANT TO STAY SAFE. Make sure you and your parent or guardian trust the websites you are using. Also be careful about what information you post publicly. Never give your full name, age, or address to anyone without a parent or guardian's permission.

If in doubt about what to share or not to share, ask! A parent or other responsible adult can help you sort it out.

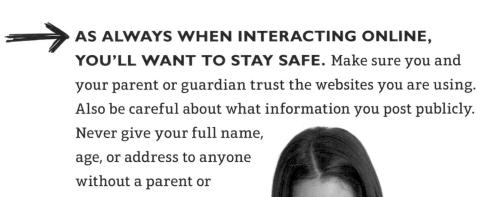

SHAWN MENDES

Shawn Mendes was fourteen when he began posting videos to YouTube and Vine, a site where users posted six-second videos. Mendes built a fast following. Fans couldn't wait for the next video! Mendes released an album in 2015 and went on tour in 2016. He credits his early success with being able to reach so many people so quickly via the Internet.

Playing, creating, and recording music is fun—and being able to share music with friends, family, and people around the world is an exciting way to improve both your musical and your technical skills. Are you ready to try it? Then it's time to put your talents into action!

♫ MUSIC-MAKING CHECKLIST

ARE YOU READY TO START MAKING AND SHARING MUSIC? Here's a simple breakdown of some steps that might help you to write, record, and share your songs.

1. Come up with a topic for your song. You can sing about a person, an idea, or even a story you heard that inspired you.
2. Write your lyrics. Come up with verses and a chorus for your song.
3. Write a melody to go with your lyrics.
4. Decide how many musicians you want to perform your song. Gather all the musicians you'll need. Find a quiet, empty room to record your music.
5. Gather all the equipment you'll need, such as a microphone, headphones, and a good music software program.

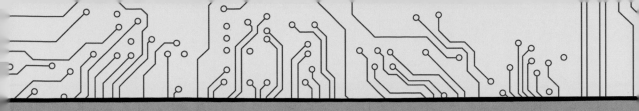

6. Start recording. First, make a scratch track. Then record each instrument and singer separately.

7. Make sure people are happy with the music they've created. If something doesn't sound right, record that part again.

8. Edit the tracks, choosing the best ones to make sure your final song sounds polished. Then edit the song to eliminate any unwanted noises and to adjust the sound to your liking.

9. Decide how you want to share your music. Do you want only your friends to see it, or are you ready for a bigger audience? Make sure your parent or guardian agrees with your decision.

10. Post your song. Adjust your privacy settings, and create keywords so others can find your music. Share the links to your song with friends and family.

11. Build a bigger audience if you choose to by doing things like thanking people who leave comments on your work.

12. Create more music to build your skills as a musician.

GLOSSARY

chorus: a part of a song that is repeated between verses

covers: performances of songs that have been written and performed by other musicians

lyrics: the words of a song

melody: the main tune in a piece of music

tracks: recorded layers of sound that are combined to form songs

verses: sections of a song that tell that song's story

vocals: singing parts in a piece of music

FURTHER INFORMATION

Alessia Cara Biography
http://www.kidzworld.com/article/29816-alessia-cara-biography

Caravantes, Peggy. *Shawn Mendes: Pop Star*. Mankato, MN: Child's World, 2017.

How to Write Songs
http://www.kidzworld.com/article/24798-how-to-write-songs

Lindeen, Mary. *Smart Online Communication: Protecting Your Digital Footprint*. Minneapolis: Lerner Publications, 2016.

Mara, Wil. *Sound Engineer*. Ann Arbor, MI: Cherry Lake, 2016.

Online Safety
https://kids.usa.gov/online-safety/index.shtml

Social Networking
http://www.kidsmart.org.uk/socialnetworking

INDEX

chorus, 10

editing, 5, 12, 15

keywords, 20–21

lyrics, 7–11

melody, 6, 8–9

social media, 16, 18

software, 11
song structure, 10

tracks, 12–13

verses, 10
vocals, 13, 15

YouTube, 19–20

PHOTO ACKNOWLEDGMENTS

The images in this book are used with the permission of: iStockphoto.com/Eshma, p. 4; © Dan Anderson/ZUMAPRESS.com/ImageCollect, p. 5; iStockphoto.com/iprogressman, p. 6; iStockphoto.com/Cronislaw, p. 7; iStockphoto.com/shironosov, p. 9; iStockphoto.com/joakimbkk, p. 11; iStock.com/arieliona, p. 12; iStockphoto.com/SolStock, p. 13; iStockphoto.com/grandriver, p. 14; iStock.com/fstop123, p. 15; nevodka/Shutterstock.com, p. 16; iStockphoto.com/kali9, p. 17 (top); iStockphoto.com/Mike_Kiev, p. 17 (bottom); arek_malang/Shutterstock.com, p. 18; JStone/Shutterstock.com, p. 19; Ralph Arvesen/Flickr (CC BY 2.0), p. 20; iStockphoto.com/AlekZotoff, p. 21; iStock.com/zeljkosantrac, p. 22; NatashaFedorova/Deposit Photos, p. 23; © Yakub88/Dreamstime.com, p. 24; iStockphoto.com/FatCamera, p. 25; iStock.com/jhorrocks, p. 26; StarMaxWorldwide/ImageCollect, p. 27; DESIGN ELEMENTS: Iliveinoctober/Shutterstock.com; iStockphoto.com/fonikum; iStockphoto.com/Sylverarts; iStockphoto.com/chaluk; iStockphoto.com/pixaroma; iStockphoto.com/chekat; iStockphoto.com/ulimi; iStockphoto.com/slalom.

Cover: Peathegee Inc/Blend Images/Getty Images.